NO LONGER PROPERTY OF
ANYTHINK LIBRARIES/
RANGEVIEW LIBRARY DISTRICT

D0460683

MIRACLES OF MEDICINE

ANESTHETICS

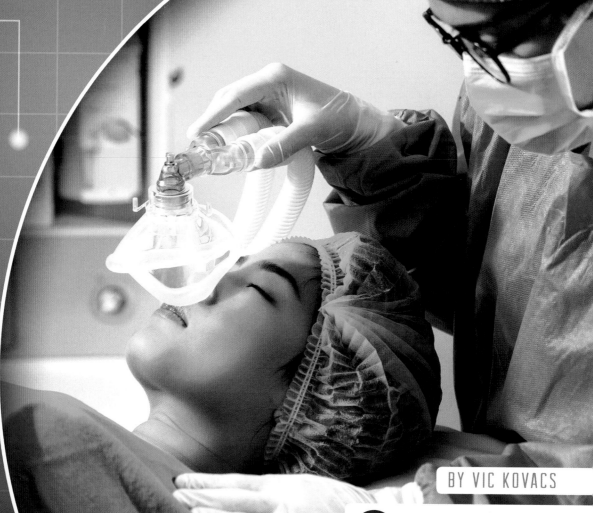

BY VIC KOVACS

Gareth Stevens
PUBLISHING

Please visit our website, www.garethstevens.com.
For a free color catalog of all our high-quality books, call toll free 1-800-542-2595 or fax 1-877-542-2596.

Cataloging-in-Publication Data

Names: Kovacs, Vic.
Title: Anesthetics / Vic Kovacs.
Description: New York : Gareth Stevens Publishing, 2017. | Series: Miracles of medicine | Includes index.
Identifiers: ISBN 9781482460933 (pbk.) | ISBN 9781482461619 (library bound) |
    ISBN 9781482460940 (6 pack)
Subjects: LCSH: Anesthesia--Juvenile literature. | Anesthetics--Juvenile literature.
Classification: LCC RD81.K68 2017 | DDC 617.96--dc23

Published in 2017 by
Gareth Stevens Publishing
111 East 14th Street, Suite 349
New York, NY 10003

Copyright © 2017 Gareth Stevens Publishing

Developed and produced for Rosen by BlueApple*Works* Inc.

Managing Editor for BlueApple*Works*: Melissa McClellan
Designer: Joshua Avramson
Photo Research: Jane Reid
Editor: Marcia Abramson

Photo Credits: VectorLifestylepic/Shutterstock; Title page VectorLifestylepic/Shutterstock; p. 5, 7, 9 Wellcome Images/Creative Commons; p. Public Domain; p. 8 Julius Giere/Public Domain; p. 11, 17, 30, 36, 37, 39, 41 Tyler Olson/Shutterstock; p. 12, 13, 31 ChaNaWiT/Shutterstock; p. 15 Dmitry Kalinovsky/Shutterstock; p. 18 Romaset/Shutterstock; p. 19 Alex Cherepanov/Shutterstock; p. 20 MrArifnajafov/Creative Commons; p. 21 edwardolive/Shutterstock; p. 22 Anna Baburkina/Shutterstock; p. 23 Dreams Come True/Shutterstock; p. 25 beerkoff/Shutterstock; p. 26 Firma V/Shutterstock; p. 27 ProStockStudio/Shutterstock; p. 28 l i g h t p o e t /Shutterstock; p. 29 Samrith Na Lumpoon/Shutterstock; p. 32 VILevi/Shutterstock; p. 33 wavebreakmedia/Shutterstock; p. 35 DiverDave/Creative Commons; p. 43 sima/Shutterstock

All rights reserved. No part of this book may be reproduced in any form without permission from the publisher, except by a reviewer.

Printed in the United States of America
CPSIA compliance information: Batch CW17GS: For further information contact Gareth Stevens, New York, New York at 1-800-542-2595.

CONTENTS

CHAPTER 1

THE HISTORY OF ANESTHETICS

Throughout history, human beings have tried to find substances that were capable of dulling pain. Without such a substance, **surgery** was viewed as a painful and dangerous last resort. After all, if a patient was awake and able to feel every cut and movement, the pain was often too much to bear.

One of the earliest substances used to dull pain was opium. Opium is a drug that is made using seed pods from the opium poppy plant. There is some evidence to indicate that it was being used as a painkiller as far back as 3400 BC by the ancient Sumerians. Opium remained in use for thousands of years. Even today, some drugs containing opium are still prescribed. These kinds of drugs are called opiates.

SENSATION-FREE

THE TERM "ANESTHETIC" WAS COINED BY OLIVER WENDELL HOLMES, AN AMERICAN DOCTOR, IN 1846. IT COMES FROM THE GREEK, AND MEANS "WITHOUT SENSATION." IN 1902, DR. MATHIAS J. SEIFERT CAME UP WITH THE TERMS "ANESTHESIOLOGY" FOR THE FIELD AND "ANESTHESIOLOGIST" FOR AN EXPERT IN THAT FIELD.

After the breakthroughs presented by ether and chloroform, the study of anesthetics took off. The 20th century saw the development of a variety of new drugs. New methods of administering drugs were also pioneered. 1923 saw the first use of an ethylene-oxygen mixture that would continue to see use for the next three decades. Sodium thiopental was developed during the 1930s, and was injected instead of being inhaled like most anesthetics up to that point. It's better known today under another name: truth serum. Lidocaine, a fast-acting numbing agent, was discovered in 1946, and made available for sale two years later. It is still in use today in many dental surgeries.

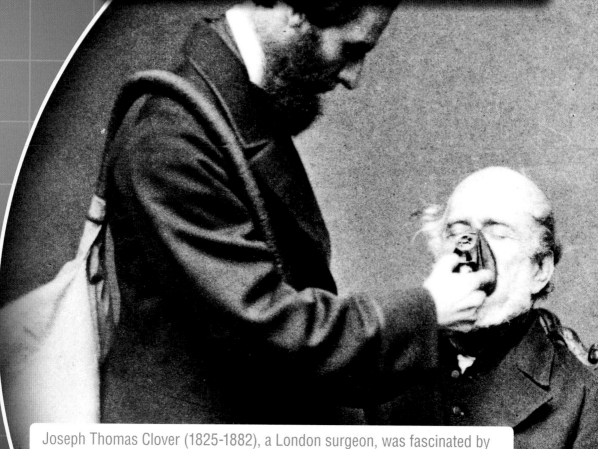

Joseph Thomas Clover (1825-1882), a London surgeon, was fascinated by the discovery of anesthetics. He decided to specialize in this new field of medicine and invented an ether inhaler and chloroform apparatus, which he is shown demonstrating on his father. He often was called to treat famous patients such as the Prince and Princess of Wales and Florence Nightingale.

Other cultures experimented with various herbs and narcotics to help deal with pain. Some of these included hemlock, mandragora, and cannabis smoke. Alcohol also has a long history of surgical use. Some doctors even used potions that combined herbs or opium in wine, which must have had quite an effect!

Other than drugs and herbal concoctions, certain techniques were employed to make surgery bearable. Tourniquets would be tied around a limb to cut off the blood supply so it would become numb. In China, acupuncture developed over the centuries as a therapeutic treatment.

In the 1840s, a new anesthetic technique was gaining traction in England: hypnotism. After attending a few shows that demonstrated "animal magnetism," Scottish surgeon James Braid became fascinated by the subject. After several experiments in which he was able to place himself under hypnosis, he developed a technique to do the same to others. As this technique became more widespread, some doctors began to use it to produce a trance in their patients that would allow them to endure surgery. The most prolific of these practitioners was Dr. James Esdaile, who performed over 300 such procedures in both England and India. However, the practice became less popular as new discoveries were made in the field of anesthesia.

Scottish surgeon James Braid (1785-1860) coined the term "hypnosis" and applied scientific principles to investigating it, such as studying meditation and yoga techniques.

Nitrous oxide, also known as laughing gas, became very popular as a dental anesthetic in the 1860s. It was administered through a simple breathing bag made of rubber cloth. Hospitals of the time also used it to relax patients before giving ether or chloroform.

One of the first important discoveries in modern anesthesiology was the discovery of nitrous oxide in 1772 by the scientist Joseph Priestley. Priestley also discovered oxygen and invented soda water. In 1800, a young British scientist named Humphry Davy published his findings on the gas, noting that it could relieve pain and might be useful for surgery. However, his findings were largely ignored until 1844. In the meantime, members of the British upper class began using the gas for its **euphoric** effects. They would throw "laughing gas parties," where it would be inhaled and sometimes cause the inhaler to giggle uncontrollably.

Opium was still commonly used as a medication in the early 19th century. However, its effectiveness was highly variable. Friedrich Sertürner, a pharmacist's assistant in Germany, decided to try to correct this. He attempted to isolate the active ingredient in the plant, so that standard doses could be given. This would allow the drug to be administered with much more reliable results. Working at night at the pharmacy where he was an apprentice, he managed to distill a yellow-white crystal by placing opium in **ammoniated** water

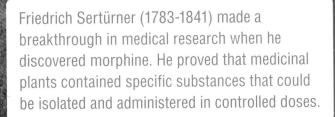

Friedrich Sertürner (1783-1841) made a breakthrough in medical research when he discovered morphine. He proved that medicinal plants contained specific substances that could be isolated and administered in controlled doses.

He first tested this substance on dogs, which died. After adjusting the dose, he named the drug after Morpheus, the Greek god of dreams. However, so that the name was similar to other drugs of the time, it was changed to morphine. Because Sertürner didn't have any medical training, his discovery wasn't accepted at first. However, after continued experiments on himself and local children produced consistently safe results, it began to catch on. The drug's abilities to relieve pain and induce sleep were desperately needed, and it became widely available by the 1820s.

Surgical anesthetics did not see regular use until the mid-1800s. Up until then, the only commonly used substances to prepare patients for surgery were alcohol and opium. However, both had their problems. Opium was sometimes very effective, but occasionally not, depending on the batch. Alcohol often led to vomiting and other issues. Ether is a colorless, extremely flammable liquid that had been around for hundreds of years. However, it wasn't until the 1840s that doctors attempted to use it as an anesthetic.

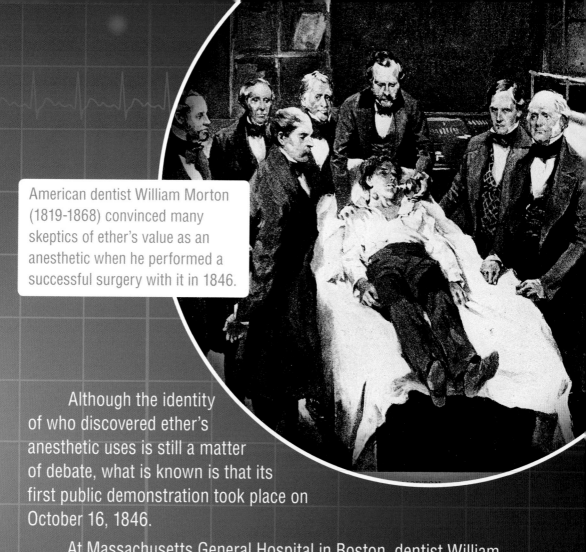

American dentist William Morton (1819-1868) convinced many skeptics of ether's value as an anesthetic when he performed a successful surgery with it in 1846.

Although the identity of who discovered ether's anesthetic uses is still a matter of debate, what is known is that its first public demonstration took place on October 16, 1846.

At Massachusetts General Hospital in Boston, dentist William Morton administered ether vapors to his patient Gilbert Abbott. With Abbott safely unconscious, Morton successfully removed a tumor from his neck.

The following year saw the first use of chloroform as an anesthetic. The Scottish doctor James Simpson was the first to use the sweet-smelling, colorless liquid on a human, and it became very popular throughout Europe and eventually America. However, chloroform did have drawbacks. An improper dose could kill a patient, and it led to a number of **fatalities**. As safer anesthetics were developed, both ether and chloroform use were phased out.

CHAPTER 2

HOW ANESTHETICS WORK

Anesthetics are a type of drug whose main purpose is to stop sensation. They are most often used to prevent pain. Anesthetics are what allow most modern surgeries to be performed. Without them, the pain experienced by the patient would simply be too great for the surgery to happen. Different types of anesthetics have different effects. Some cause numbness, others prevent the patient from moving, and still others cause full unconsciousness. Some even cause amnesia, or memory loss!

Anesthetics generally function by getting in the way of the body's central nervous system. This system connects the millions of nerve endings in the human body. When an anesthetic is administered, it makes contact with nerve endings through the bloodstream, organ tissues, and fat in the skin.

GOING UNDER

ANESTHESIA USUALLY BEGINS WITH A MILD DRUG TO HELP THE PATIENT RELAX AND FEEL SLEEPY. THIS CAN BE ADMINISTERED THROUGH INJECTION OR A BREATHING MASK. PATIENTS OFTEN DO NOT EVEN REMEMBER THIS PHASE. AS A STRONGER ANESTHETIC IS GIVEN, THE PATIENT FALLS TRULY UNCONSCIOUS. WHEN DOCTORS THEN INSERT A TUBE INTO THE WINDPIPE AND PROCEED WITH SURGERY, THE PATIENT NEVER NOTICES.

Anesthesia awareness is a very rare, but incredibly horrifying complication that sometimes occurs under general anesthesia. Sometimes, patients are not given enough anesthetic to keep them unconscious, but are given enough to keep them paralyzed and unable to communicate. In these cases, patients are aware of the surgery being performed on them, but cannot do anything to stop it. In certain extreme cases, they're even able to feel pain. Luckily, less than 1 percent of patients experience this ordeal.

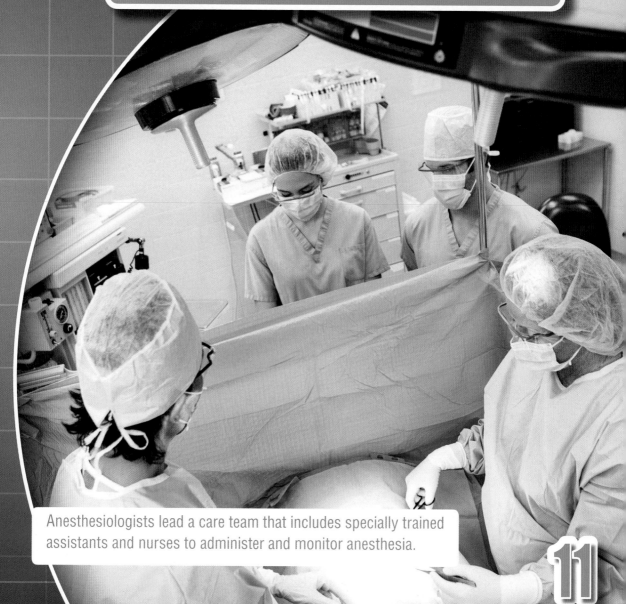

Anesthesiologists lead a care team that includes specially trained assistants and nurses to administer and monitor anesthesia.

Some anesthetics target specific groups of nerves for different operations. These nerve clusters are responsible for relaying pain signals from one part of the body to the brain. For example, if you're having a cavity filled, you would want the pain receptors from your mouth to be blocked. After all, if your mouth is sending pain signals to your brain, it wouldn't do much good to block the nerves in your foot, would it? Other anesthetics render the patient totally unconscious. These are generally reserved for larger procedures that it would be unpleasant to be awake for, like organ transplants.

ADMINISTERING ANESTHETICS

Different anesthetics are administered in different ways. There are four main methods of administering them. Internally administered anesthetics are usually swallowed, but they might enter the body in another way. However they are taken, they pass through the body's digestive system. Common forms for this type of anesthetic include pills and tablets. These drugs are limited by something called the first pass effect, which is how much of the medicine is removed when it passes through the liver, before it can enter the bloodstream and move through the rest of the body.

Once an intravenous (IV) line has been started, anesthesia and other medicine can be delivered quickly into the bloodstream. This also avoids additional needle sticks!

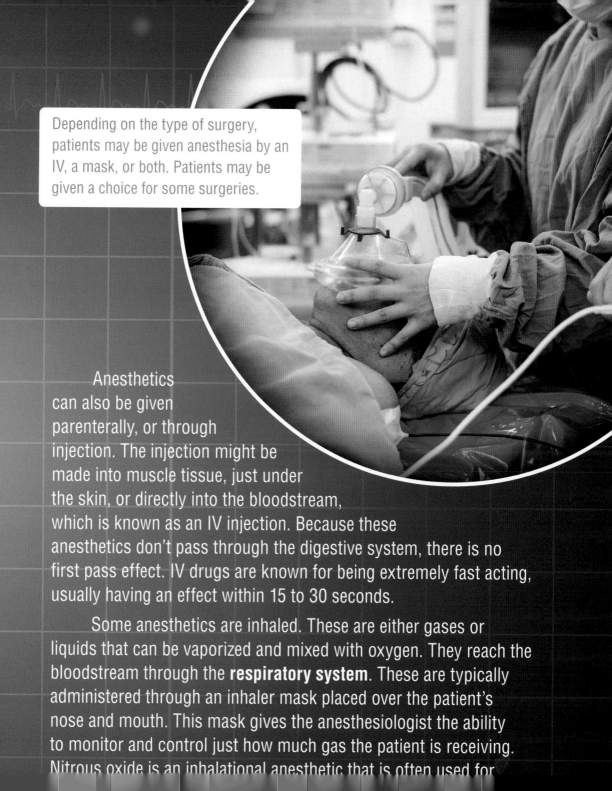

Depending on the type of surgery, patients may be given anesthesia by an IV, a mask, or both. Patients may be given a choice for some surgeries.

Anesthetics can also be given parenterally, or through injection. The injection might be made into muscle tissue, just under the skin, or directly into the bloodstream, which is known as an IV injection. Because these anesthetics don't pass through the digestive system, there is no first pass effect. IV drugs are known for being extremely fast acting, usually having an effect within 15 to 30 seconds.

Some anesthetics are inhaled. These are either gases or liquids that can be vaporized and mixed with oxygen. They reach the bloodstream through the **respiratory system**. These are typically administered through an inhaler mask placed over the patient's nose and mouth. This mask gives the anesthesiologist the ability to monitor and control just how much gas the patient is receiving. Nitrous oxide is an inhalational anesthetic that is often used for

Other anesthetics are administered topically. These drugs are placed directly onto the area that needs to be anesthetized, and are absorbed by either the skin or mucous membrane. They typically take the form of creams, ointments, or lotions, but can also be sprayed on. Some are used for relatively minor afflictions, like itchy or irritated skin. Others are used in dental surgery to numb the mouth before another anesthetic is injected with a needle. Some are used to numb a person's eye in order to perform a test or remove foreign objects.

However an anesthetic is administered, it begins to take effect once it is absorbed by the body. Once the drug reaches the bloodstream, it is distributed throughout the body. It arrives at the heart, kidneys, brain, and liver first, because of the high number of blood vessels these organs possess. After that, it will eventually reach muscle and fat tissue, which have fewer blood vessels. Eventually, the drug is deconstructed by the liver and leaves the bloodstream.

HOW THE BODY REACTS TO ANESTHETICS

Once an anesthetic is absorbed by the body, it begins to bond with specific nerve clusters. These nerve clusters send pain signals to the brain as electrical impulses. Anesthetics stop these signals by blocking these impulses. Anesthetics that produce unconsciousness work by calming down electrical impulses in the brain.

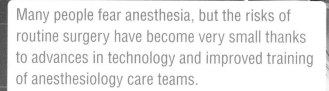

Many people fear anesthesia, but the risks of routine surgery have become very small thanks to advances in technology and improved training of anesthesiology care teams.

The brain normally communicates with itself through electrical impulses, but these are lessened under anesthesia. This means the brain isn't communicating with itself as much, which has the effect of lessening awareness, stopping the formation of memory, and/or creating a total lack of consciousness.

Although anesthetics are necessary for most surgery, they are not without risk. Different types of anesthetics have different risks. General anesthesia can cause vomiting and **nausea**, which, while unpleasant, are usually fairly mild. However, more serious side effects are possible, and can include brain or nerve damage or death in severe cases. A local anesthetic can also result in nerve damage, infection or bleeding if it is administered with a needle. Some anesthetics are injected into the spine and can cause the respiratory system to shut down if given in too large a dose.

A trained anesthesiologist is important in minimizing these risks, but risks are always present. This is because every human being is different, and it is difficult to know exactly how an individual

CHAPTER 3

LOCAL ANESTHETICS

A local anesthetic is a drug that causes a temporary lack of sensation in a particular part of the body. Some can also cause paralysis in the affected area. In the 19th century, it was discovered that the leaves from the coca plant, native to South America, had anesthetic as well as stimulative properties. Locals in Peru and Bolivia would chew on the leaves to relieve minor aches. Cocaine, a powerful drug, was first isolated from the plant in the 1850s, and was used as a local anesthetic for the first time 24 years later. However, while effective, the drug had its problems.

NATURE'S OWN

COCAINE COMES FROM THE COCA SHRUB NATIVE TO THE ANDES MOUNTAINS OF SOUTH AMERICA. IT IS ONE OF THE FEW NATURALLY OCCURRING SUBSTANCES THAT CAN BE USED AS AN ANESTHETIC, ALONG WITH OPIUM AND CURARE.

Millions of people undergo successful surgeries each year thanks to the availability of anesthesia. Before anesthetics, doctors operated only when there was no other choice, such as removing a gangrenous limb. In the early days of anesthetics, surgeons had to guess how to use ether or nitrous oxide. Today's surgeons and patients go into complex procedures with confidence in the modern anesthetic technology that makes them both painless and possible.

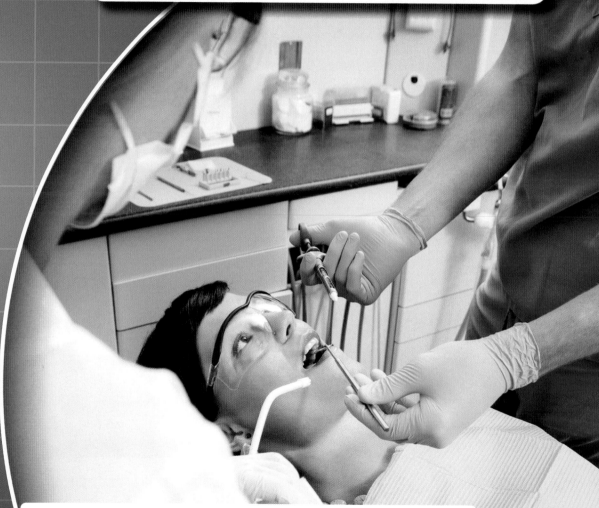

Before anesthetics, many people chose the quick pain of an extraction over the agonizing prospect of dental work. Local anesthesia allows procedures as complex as dental implants to be performed.

Cocaine was often toxic for patients, and led to several fatalities. It was also incredibly addictive. These issues led to a search for safer alternatives. Eventually, a pure form of cocaine was developed synthetically. This new artificial version didn't have the same problems when administered close to the nerves. The first injectable local anesthetic of this type was dubbed procaine. It formed the basis for all synthetic injectable local anesthetics used today.

Local anesthetics work by blocking pain signals sent from the nerves to the brain. Local anesthetics are lipid-soluble, which means that they penetrate fat tissues quickly. How quickly determines how long the drug's effects last. A highly lipid-soluble compound like ropivacaine lasts longer than lidocaine, which isn't as lipid-soluble. This just means that a higher dose of lidocaine would be needed to remain as effective as ropivacaine.

Different **biological** factors can play a part in how quickly local anesthetics take effect. For example, the narrower a person's nerve endings, the faster the effect. Also, because they are lipid-soluble, the anesthetics will travel faster if a layer of myelin, a fatty protein surrounding nerves, is present. Nerves closest to where the drug is injected are affected first, with the effect spreading out from there.

Local anesthetics usually are injected. Liquids or gels may be used for minor surgery inside the mouth, ear or on the skin's surface.

POTENTIAL PROBLEMS

In most cases, local anesthetics are safe and have few major side effects, but there are still potential risks and problems.

If it is injected, a local anesthetic may cause pain, bleeding, swelling, and even infection at the injection site. Patients may feel lightheaded and disoriented after a procedure, so they may be advised to avoid driving and making any major decisions until the effects wear off. Some patients may experience impaired movement, double vision, or slurred speech. Sometimes, local anesthetics take longer than expected to wear off. For most people, these problems resolve naturally or with prompt treatment. Surgery centers keep emergency equipment on hand just in case.

More serious problems rarely occur, but include neurological damage, strokes, seizures, and cardiac arrest. These side effects may result from an overdose of anesthetic in the bloodstream and the rest of the body. Although anesthesiologists carefully calculate how much to use, each person's metabolism and rate of absorption are different.

Allergies, especially some that are hereditary, also can cause serious reactions to local anesthetics. Doctors need to review each patient's personal and family medical history in advance to identify this and other potential problems.

REGIONAL ANESTHETICS

Regional anesthesia is the practice of using local anesthetics to block sensation from a larger area of the body than they normally would. This is different than typical local anesthetics, which only prevent sensation from a fairly small area. For example, while a local anesthetic might be used to numb part of the jaw, regional anesthetics are used to numb a larger area of the face. However, the patient still remains conscious and awake. They might be given a **sedative** to help them remain calm. Two of the main fields that local anesthetics are used in are dentistry and obstetrics, the field of medicine concerned with childbirth.

Two of the main techniques used for regional anesthesia are peripheral nerve blocks and spinal analgesia. Peripheral nerve blocks target specific nerve clusters that provide sensation to one region of the body, usually a limb like an arm or a leg. Spinal analgesia is a process in which an injection is made directly into an exact spot in the spine. It produces numbness from the rib cage downwards, blocking sensation from the lower half of the body. A similar technique is called an epidural.

For epidural and spinal blocks, a local anesthetic is injected directly into the back near the spinal cord. This technique blocks pain from an entire region, such as the belly or legs.

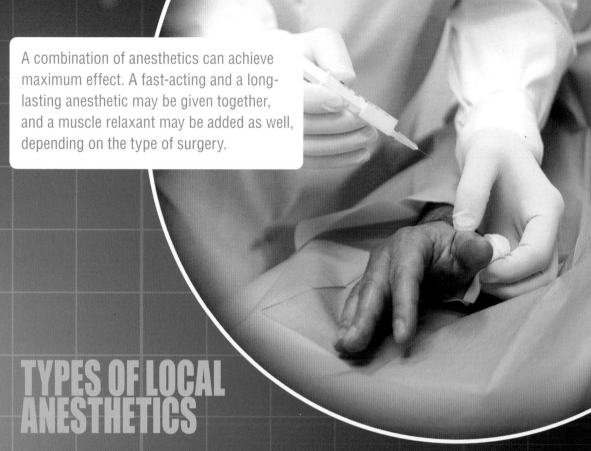

A combination of anesthetics can achieve maximum effect. A fast-acting and a long-lasting anesthetic may be given together, and a muscle relaxant may be added as well, depending on the type of surgery.

TYPES OF LOCAL ANESTHETICS

Local anesthetics generally fall into one of two categories: amino esters and amino amides. The main difference between the two is the makeup of their chemical structures, but there are other differences as well. Esters are somewhat less stable than amides. This means that they can't be stored for as long before they start to degrade.

A number of commonly used anesthetics are amino esters. The first synthetic local anesthetic, procaine, is one. Even though it was developed over a hundred years ago, it is still used for a number of purposes today. These include nerve block techniques and dental procedures. It is usually injected, and begins working quickly, in under five minutes. Its effects typically last for about an hour. It is probably better known under the trade name Novocaine.

Tetracaine is an ester anesthetic that comes in a number of forms. As a topical gel, it is used to numb the skin. As an injection, it is used most often for spinal anesthesia. It is also available as eye drops, which are administered before some procedures.

Chloroprocaine is an IV drug that causes blood vessels to constrict, unlike many other local anesthetics. This has the effect of decreasing blood loss. For this reason, it is often used during childbirth.

Benzocaine is a local anesthetic that isn't particularly strong. Because of this, it isn't used for surgical procedures. Instead, it is used topically to relieve minor discomfort from annoyances such as sunburn, bug bites, and other skin irritations. It is also an active ingredient in many cough drops used to relieve a sore throat.

The most used amide anesthetic is lidocaine. It is extremely versatile, and can be applied in a variety of ways. Often injected, it can also be applied topically as a cream, or sometimes even a patch. In dentistry, it has mostly taken the place of procaine, and is used as an anesthetic for the most common dental procedures. These include cavity fillings, tooth extractions, and root canals. Scientists developing new local anesthetics tend to focus more on amino-amides, because they are more stable and longer-lasting than esters. They also provoke fewer **allergic reactions**.

Cosmetic surgery is another area of medicine that has benefited from the availability of local anesthetics.

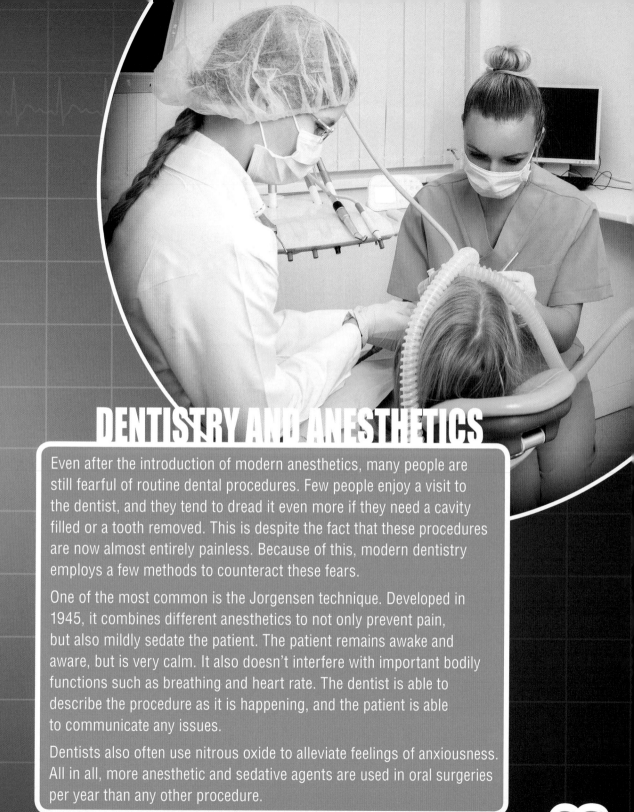

DENTISTRY AND ANESTHETICS

Even after the introduction of modern anesthetics, many people are still fearful of routine dental procedures. Few people enjoy a visit to the dentist, and they tend to dread it even more if they need a cavity filled or a tooth removed. This is despite the fact that these procedures are now almost entirely painless. Because of this, modern dentistry employs a few methods to counteract these fears.

One of the most common is the Jorgensen technique. Developed in 1945, it combines different anesthetics to not only prevent pain, but also mildly sedate the patient. The patient remains awake and aware, but is very calm. It also doesn't interfere with important bodily functions such as breathing and heart rate. The dentist is able to describe the procedure as it is happening, and the patient is able to communicate any issues.

Dentists also often use nitrous oxide to alleviate feelings of anxiousness. All in all, more anesthetic and sedative agents are used in oral surgeries per year than any other procedure.

GENERAL ANESTHETICS

General anesthetics are a type of drugs that have the effect of calming the central nervous system. This causes the patient to become unconscious, and allows surgeries to be performed that would otherwise be impossible. Other effects might include amnesia and analgesia. It also prevents the patient's protective reflexes.

The earliest modern anesthetics were general anesthetics. Ether was the first of these, and was very effective. The fumes given off by ether were so powerful that they completely knocked out early patients. However, inhaling the gas was not considered very pleasant. Ether was also volatile, and was known to burst into flame or explode. As a result, doctors were searching for an alternative. One contender was chloroform. It was less volatile than ether, and had much the same effect.

ROYALTY'S FAVORITE

CHLOROFORM BECAME SO POPULAR IN EUROPE IN THE 1850S QUEEN VICTORIA USED IT DURING THE BIRTH OF HER FINAL TWO CHILDREN!

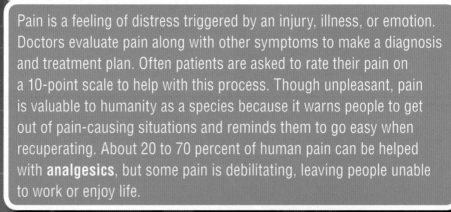

Pain is a feeling of distress triggered by an injury, illness, or emotion. Doctors evaluate pain along with other symptoms to make a diagnosis and treatment plan. Often patients are asked to rate their pain on a 10-point scale to help with this process. Though unpleasant, pain is valuable to humanity as a species because it warns people to get out of pain-causing situations and reminds them to go easy when recuperating. About 20 to 70 percent of human pain can be helped with **analgesics**, but some pain is debilitating, leaving people unable to work or enjoy life.

General anesthesia requires close monitoring because of its widespread effect on the body. A screen displays sensor readings for pulse, blood pressure, blood gases, temperature, and heart activity.

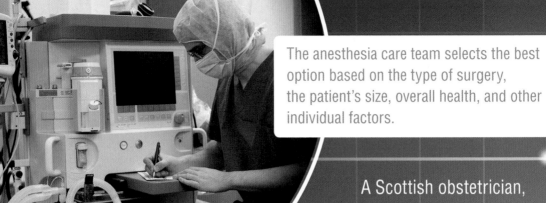

The anesthesia care team selects the best option based on the type of surgery, the patient's size, overall health, and other individual factors.

A Scottish obstetrician, James Simpson, popularized chloroform's use, and began using it to deliver babies in 1847. It also saw use during surgery and other medical procedures. Unfortunately, just a year later, tragedy struck. During a toenail extraction, a 15-year-old girl died while under the effects of chloroform. This led to a wider awareness of the dangers associated with the drug. Stories were reported of people using it for abductions and even more horrible crimes. With more and more patients dying, the drug was considered too dangerous by the early 20th century. It is no longer used as a medical anesthetic.

TYPES OF ANESTHETICS

There are two types of general anesthetics: gases and IVs. Within these categories, there are several different unique anesthetic agents. Often, a state of general anesthesia is achieved by using a combination of gases and IV drugs. The exact anesthetics used depend on a number of factors including the procedure being performed and the patient's medical history.

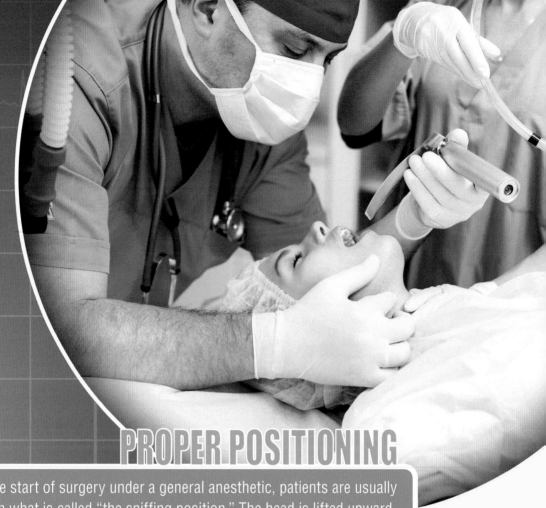

PROPER POSITIONING

At the start of surgery under a general anesthetic, patients are usually put in what is called "the sniffing position." The head is lifted upward about four inches (10 cm) so the patient seems to be sniffing the air. This keeps the mouth, pharynx, larynx, and trachea in a straight alignment that allows tubing to be inserted with minimal resistance. People naturally use this position, with head forward and slightly tilted back, when they are out of breath.

Once patients are unconscious, doctors and nurses put their body in the best position for the surgery being performed. Patients may be on their back, side, or belly, sitting up, in a jackknife position, or in a variation of one of these. Whatever the position, it is chosen to provide the best access for surgeons while keeping the patient's airway open for breathing and anesthetic administration.

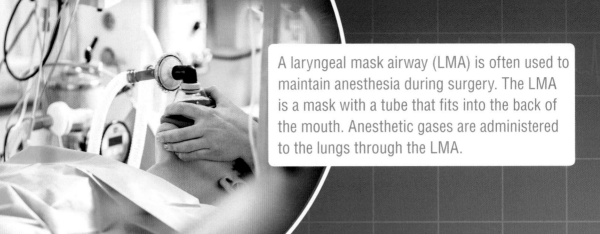

A laryngeal mask airway (LMA) is often used to maintain anesthesia during surgery. The LMA is a mask with a tube that fits into the back of the mouth. Anesthetic gases are administered to the lungs through the LMA.

GASES

Inhalation is one of the two methods used to administer general anesthetics. The patient will breathe in a gas that then begins to take effect. There are two kinds of inhaled anesthetics. The first is nitrous oxide, which causes a patient to become calm, and makes any pain less noticeable. The second consists of halogenated agents, of which there are several. They produce effects similar to those of chloroform and ether, but are safer and less volatile.

Nitrous oxide was first discovered in the 1770s by Sir Joseph Priestley. Despite discovering it, Priestley wasn't quite sure what to do with it, and it took the work of subsequent scientists to realize its full potential. By the 1840s, there were traveling road shows dedicated to exhibiting the effects of nitrous oxide. In 1844, one such demonstration in Connecticut was attended by the dentist Horace Wells. Wells noticed that one of the volunteers testing the gas hurt his leg, but when asked about it afterwards was completely unaware that he had.

Some patients need help breathing
and inhaling anesthetics. A mechanical
ventilator is used in these cases.

Intrigued, Wells decided
to experiment on himself to see
if nitrous oxide could be used to
numb pain during dental surgery.
After inhaling nitrous oxide, he had his
fellow dentist John Riggs extract one of
his teeth. The operation was painless, and Wells
quickly began using the gas as an anesthetic in his dental practice. By
the 1860s, it had been widely adopted across the field of dentistry,
where it remains in use today.

From its introduction in 1956 until the 1980s, halothane was one
of the most commonly used halogenated gasses for anesthetic purposes.
When it first became available, it was considered much safer than
previous anesthetics. It eliminated the flammability of ether, and wasn't
nearly as toxic as chloroform. However, it eventually fell out of favor in
the United States when it was discovered that it was toxic to the liver.
Despite this, its affordability means it is still often used in less wealthy
countries. A similar gas is sevoflurane. It is much less irritating to the
throat than other halogenated gasses, which cuts down on negative
side effects such as coughing. It is fast acting, with patients becoming
unconscious within about two minutes. It also has a shorter recovery
time compared to halothane, with patients waking up fairly quickly once
it starts to lose effect. However, because they're waking up so quickly,
patients sometimes wake up confused or upset.

INTRAVENOUS ANESTHETICS

General anesthetics that are injected into the bloodstream are known as intravenous, or IV anesthetics. There are others that are injected into muscle or just under the skin, but they aren't used as often. This is because they tend to be more painful and act less quickly than IV anesthetics. There are two main methods of administering IV anesthetics: either they are injected with a needle, or they are delivered using an IV drip, which is a bag with a drug mixture that is connected to a vein. Like some local anesthetics, IV anesthetics are typically lipid-soluble. This helps them work quickly. After being delivered to the spine and the brain through the bloodstream, they're absorbed by cell membranes that are composed of fat in those areas.

The development of IV anesthetics was dependent on the introduction of new technology in the early 1900s. One of these developments was the popularization of the syringe, a type of needle connected to a hollow chamber that could be filled with drugs or other injectable substances. Around the same time, advances were being made with IV systems. These new technologies allowed drugs to be administered in a way that wasn't possible before.

A syringe is a simple pump with a plunger, which is pulled up to fill the syringe and pushed down to inject the contents, such as an anesthetic.

Researchers began to create drugs that could take advantage of these new technologies. There are a number of IV drugs that are commonly used for anesthetic purposes today. The most popular include propofol, ketamine, etomidate, dexmedetomidine, and a type of drugs called barbiturates.

Propofol is the most widely used IV drug for general anesthetic purposes currently. Although it works quickly and effectively, it also causes lowered blood pressure and suppresses respiratory function, which means it requires careful observation during use. Ketamine does not have these drawbacks, which makes it popular for use in children, as well as patients with respiratory or heart issues. Although it is often administered intravenously, it can also be taken orally, nasally, rectally, or injected into muscle tissue. This makes it a fairly versatile general anesthetic. Etomidate doesn't affect the heart and lungs as much as propofol, but it has other drawbacks, including an inability to stop dangerous convulsions, as well as a higher rate of side effects such as nausea and vomiting post-surgery. Dexmedetomidine is a relatively new drug that is effective in relieving pain while also sedating a patient. It causes breathing to slow, but less so than other drugs. It does cause a drop in heart rate, though.

It takes skill to start an IV line properly, which is done by placing a small needle into a vein. Then the sharp part of the needle is removed and replaced by a plastic tube which can be used for administration of medicines including anesthetics.

Barbiturates are a type of IV anesthetics that were first developed in the late 1800s. This makes them some of the earliest used IV anesthetics. They work by depressing the central nervous system, and were typically used to help sedate and calm patients. Although they were the most popular type of IV anesthetics until the 1990s, they did have a few serious downsides. One was that they severely affect breathing, slowing respiratory rates. They can also be very addictive. Also, they do not possess strong analgesic properties, making them ineffective at combating pain. They eventually became less widely used as propofol became a popular alternative.

COMPLICATIONS AND SIDE EFFECTS

General anesthesia is usually very safe, but it can lead to complications or negative side effects. These side effects are somewhat more likely to occur after being placed under general anesthesia than after local or regional anesthesia, because general anesthesia affects the whole body. Most of these side effects are fairly minor, but more severe ones do occur at times.

Minor side effects can include nausea, vomiting, achy muscles, itchy skin, and chills.

The care team must adjust the dosage quickly if a patient becomes too deeply anesthetized.

Constant and careful monitoring allows the anesthesiology team to adjust dosages should a patient develop serious side effects, such as decreased heart rate or blood pressure, which could be fatal.

Confusion also sometimes occurs after regaining consciousness, and can sometimes last for days or even weeks. This usually only occurs in older patients, though. Often during surgery, a breathing tube is inserted into the patient's throat, and this can cause soreness afterwards.

More severe side effects are much more rare, but might include delirium or cognitive dysfunction, such as memory loss or difficulty concentrating or learning.

Severe complications only occur in about one in 10,000 cases, but when they do, they can be very dangerous. A patient might suffer a serious allergic reaction to an anesthetic, or might experience a stroke, heart attack, or serious brain damage. In very rare cases the patient might experience anesthetic awareness, where they're conscious of the operation being performed on them but are still too sedated to do anything. Lastly, death does sometimes occur under general anesthesia, but it is exceedingly rare, only occuring about once out of every 100,000 patients at most.

ANESTHETIC TECHNOLOGY

Making sure that anesthetics are administered properly takes a lot of careful work and planning. While the exact operation being performed is a major factor in determining the type of anesthetic to use, every patient is different. Because of this, everyone goes through something called a preoperative evaluation, which is a review of both a patient's medical history and their current health. This helps the doctor determine exactly what type of anesthetic should be used, and helps reduce potential side effects and complications, both during and after surgery. After all, it would be dangerous to give a patient with a heart condition an anesthetic that severely lowers their heart rate.

DAMMIS

ANESTHESIOLOGISTS USE A SHORTHAND TO HELP THEM REMEMBER ALL THE COMPLEX STEPS OF THEIR JOB. DAMMIS IS A MNEMONIC DEVICE, OR MEMORY TOOL. THE MADE-UP WORD CONTAINS ONE LETTER FOR EACH OF THE FACTORS THAT MUST BE CHECKED CONSTANTLY. DRUGS, AIRWAY, MACHINE, MONITORS, IV LINE, AND SUCTION

Premedication usually takes place one to three hours before the administration of a general anesthetic, when patients waiting for surgery are given drugs to help them relax. The practice developed in the early days of anesthetics to help patients tolerate the intense vapors of chloroform or ether. Today, some patients choose to skip premedication, but many prefer to head into the operating room in a relaxed, sleepy state.

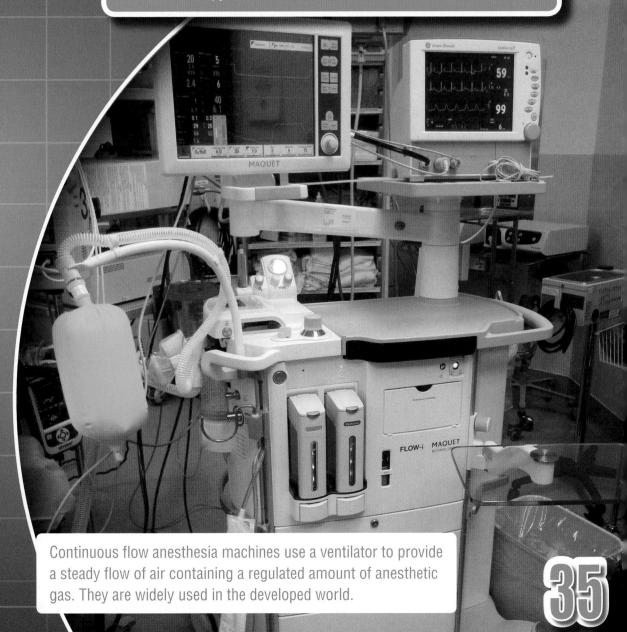

Continuous flow anesthesia machines use a ventilator to provide a steady flow of air containing a regulated amount of anesthetic gas. They are widely used in the developed world.

ANESTHESIOLOGIST

An anesthesiologist is a doctor who specializes in providing anesthesia to patients during surgery, as well as other medical procedures that require it. They undergo extensive training, and are experts in human physiology, with a deep knowledge of how the body's internal organs work and interact with each other, as well as with anesthetic drugs. They are involved with every stage of surgery from the beginning to the end.

Before surgery, a patient will meet with their anesthesiologist and will undergo a preoperative evaluation. During this, the anesthesiologist will learn about the patient's medical history, as well as any issues they might currently be dealing with. Conditions such as asthma, heart problems, diabetes, obesity, and more are all taken into account. A preexisting condition like asthma might cause the anesthesiologist to rule out a drug that suppresses respiration. The patient's overall comfort with general anesthesia is also discussed. If the idea of being placed under general anesthesia causes anxiety in the patient, the anesthesiologist might decide to give them a sedative before receiving general anesthesia. If the patient is given a sedative, it might affect the dose of anesthesia they receive afterwards, and needs to be taken into consideration.

Nurse anesthetists work on care teams or on their own, especially in rural hospitals. After receiving a regular nursing degree, they must earn a specialized master's degree, which takes 24-42 months.

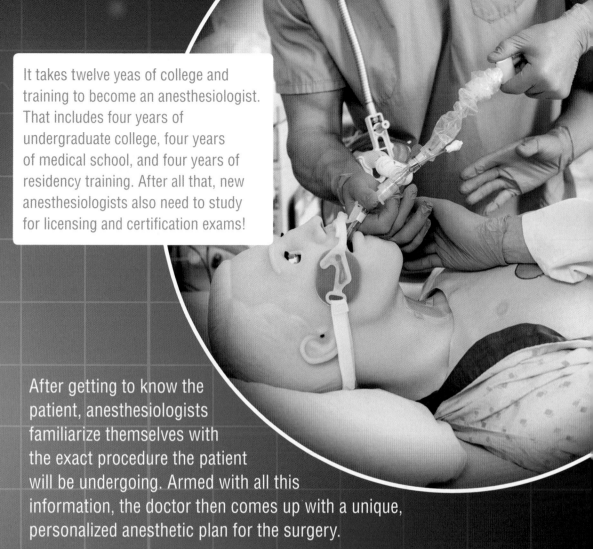

It takes twelve yeas of college and training to become an anesthesiologist. That includes four years of undergraduate college, four years of medical school, and four years of residency training. After all that, new anesthesiologists also need to study for licensing and certification exams!

After getting to know the patient, anesthesiologists familiarize themselves with the exact procedure the patient will be undergoing. Armed with all this information, the doctor then comes up with a unique, personalized anesthetic plan for the surgery.

The day of surgery, the anesthesiologist's job is to administer whatever combination of sedatives and anesthetic agents they have determined the patient will receive. They check any machines and equipment they'll be using to make sure they're working properly. After the patient has been placed under anesthesia, the anesthesiologist then monitors them carefully, watching for any change in vital signs that might indicate trouble.

After surgery, the anesthesiologist is also usually responsible for helping to manage any pain the patient might feel as a result of surgery.

They also continue to monitor the patient to ensure they don't experience any adverse effects as a result of the anesthetics they were given. It is a comprehensive job that encompasses every stage of surgery.

ANESTHETIC TECHNOLOGY

Today, anesthesiologists use a device called an anesthesia machine to assist them in surgery. It is used in procedures where the patient is given an inhaled anesthetic. It is a complex machine that combines a number of different devices for a variety of purposes. It delivers the gas, as well as oxygen, and includes a ventilator that allows the patient to continue breathing. They also incorporate a number of different monitoring devices. These allow the anesthesiologist to keep track of the patient's blood pressure, heartbeat, body temperature, and brain activity. They also monitor exactly how much anesthetic and oxygen are currently in the patient's bloodstream, as well as the amount of carbon dioxide being exhaled. All of these are watched carefully, with doctors reacting immediately if a negative change occurs. Machines are also equipped with various safety features. These include an alarm that sounds if the oxygen supply stops working, as well as an immediate shut-off feature if the proper ratio of anesthetic gases to oxygen is not being delivered. Another alarm sounds if a patient stops breathing. Because anesthetic machines are such specialized pieces of equipment, they require a trained anesthesiologist to ensure they're working and to interpret the data they're keeping track of

Patients usually spend one to two hours in a recovery room after anesthesia. As they wake up and regain function, the anesthesiology team checks on them.

RECOVERY PROCESS

After surgery, the patient is placed in a recovery room, where the effects of anesthesia begin to wear off. It's during this recovery time that most side effects present themselves, so a patient's vital signs are carefully monitored, including blood pressure, respiratory and heart rate, and the amount of oxygen and anesthetics in the system. Patients are also watched to ensure they're not disoriented, and can communicate. Once they can talk, the level of pain they're feeling is evaluated, and they may be given additional painkillers. Once a patient's vitals are at normal levels and side effects such as dizziness, nausea, and vomiting have subsided, a patient may be discharged from the hospital. Each patient is unique, though, and recovery times vary on a case by case basis. An anesthesiologist's job continues until they decide a patient has adequately recovered from anesthesia. Today, many patients can go home on the same day as their surgery. However, there are often lingering anesthetic effects, and a patient should not drive after receiving anesthesia for at least 24 hours.

ANESTHETICS OF THE FUTURE

Since the introduction of the first widely used modern anesthetics in the mid-1800s, the field has advanced by leaps and bounds. Today, surgeries that would have been too painful to imagine a hundred years ago are commonplace. However, just because things are better than they were does not mean there's no room for improvement. Researchers and scientists continue to investigate new technologies and approaches that will hopefully make anesthetics even safer and more effective.

One of the main avenues of current investigation is the possibility of altering the molecular structure of current drugs to improve them. Because these drugs already exist, it's hoped that safer, more effective versions can be developed quickly. These new versions might eliminate known negative side effects. This is part of a larger trend, in which doctors are more commonly looking into how to alter already available drugs, instead of creating completely new ones.

Nitrous oxide is not as powerful as newer anesthetics, but it has staying power. More than 200 years after its discovery, nitrous oxide is on the World Health Organization's list of essential medicines. It is often used to relax dental patients and children facing surgery, and for temporary pain relief. In many countries, nitrous oxide is a go-to anesthetic for childbirth because it wears off quickly and does not harm the fetus. Though it fell out of favor in the United States for a time, nitrous oxide has been making a comeback at birthing centers.

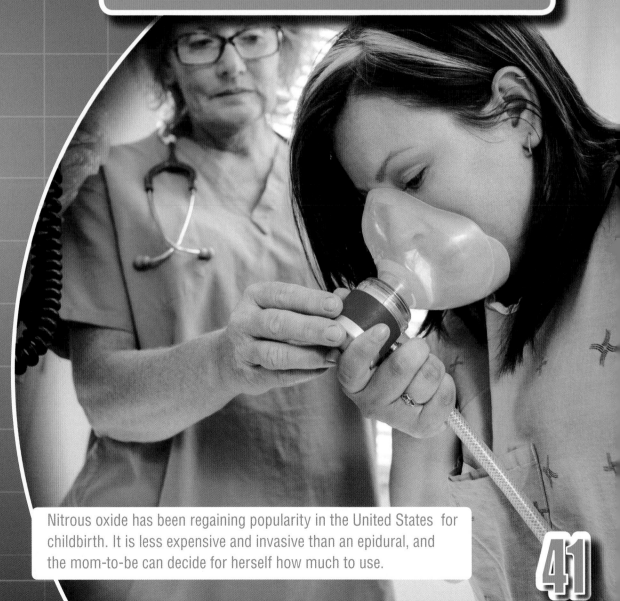

Nitrous oxide has been regaining popularity in the United States for childbirth. It is less expensive and invasive than an epidural, and the mom-to-be can decide for herself how much to use.

41

Another area of research concerns altering drugs to focus on one particular aspect of anesthesia. If drugs can be changed so that they only produce one effect, it would allow them to be combined in a way that creates exactly the state a doctor wishes to place a patient in. For example, a combination of drugs could be administered where one drug sedates the patient, another eliminates their pain, and another makes them immobile. This opens up many possibilities for allowing a patient to be at least somewhat aware and able to communicate during an operation, but leaving them calm and pain free at the same time.

Xenon is a naturally occurring gas whose anesthetic properties have been known since 1939. As of now, it is rare and costly to obtain. However, new technology might allow it to be procured at a much more reasonable cost. Also, machines that can recycle xenon are being developed. As a result, it is likely that xenon will see much wider use as a general anesthetic in the future.

As well as improving already available anesthetics, some researchers are investigating their therapeutic potential in other branches of medicine. It's possible in the future that anesthetics may be used to treat conditions as varied as infectious illness, heart disease, and even mental illness. Recent research has shown that the anesthetic ketamine might be effective as an antidepressant in patients who haven't responded to more traditional drugs. It has seen use in emergency rooms to lessen suicidal thoughts. However, much more research is necessary to determine its effectiveness and any potential side effects related to this application.

Technological devices continue to get smaller every day, and this change is reflected in anesthesiology. The application of nanotechnology, or microscopic machines, could have wide-reaching application in the field. Tiny devices might one day be linked directly to nerves, allowing them to be monitored just as heart and respiratory rates are today. This technology could also potentially be used to deliver drugs even more precisely. With higher precision, smaller doses would be needed, which lessens the likelihood of **toxicity**.

The development of anesthetics has been a true medical miracle. From common tooth extraction, to procedures like organ transplants that were almost unimaginable 150 years ago, patients requiring surgery have much less to fear today than at any other point in history. Even the miracle of childbirth has become safer and less painful as a result of their introduction. As research continues and technology advances, the field is sure to become even safer. The study of genetics opens up the possibility of tailoring anesthetics exactly to a single patient. Amidst all these changes, though, a well-trained anesthesiologist is likely to remain one of the most important resources used in a successful surgery.

Animals need anesthesia for their surgeries, too. A veterinary anesthesiologist, who has taken at least three years of special training after veterinary school, may be called in for difficult cases.

TIMELINE OF ANESTHETIC DEVELOPMENT

Friedrich Sertürner creates morphine from a pure distillation of opium from poppies.

1805

Evidence suggests that ancient Sumerians were using opium as a painkiller around this time.

3400 BC

William Morton performs the first public demonstration of ether as an anesthetic at Massachusetts General Hospital on October 16.

1846

British scientist Joseph Priestley discovers nitrous oxide, which he initially calls phlogisticated nitrous air.

1772

1844

Dentist Horace Wells successfully tests the anesthetic properties of nitrous oxide on himself.

Scottish doctor James
Simpson begins giving
chloroform to female patients
going through labor.

1847

1956

Halothane gas
is introduced for
medical practice.

1948

Lidocaine begins to
see widespread use.

1989

Propofol, today one
of the most widely
used anesthetics,
is made available in
the United States.

1912

After a number of deaths, chloroform
is deemed "too risky to use" by
the American Medical Committee
Association on Anesthesia.

GLOSSARY

allergic reaction: An immune response to harmless or beneficial foreign substances entering the body.

ammoniated: Combined or otherwise treated with ammonia, a strong-smelling, dangerous chemical.

analgesic: A drug that dulls or relieves pain.

biological: Relating to living organisms.

euphoric: Causing great joy.

fatalities: Deaths.

nausea: An uncomfortable feeling in the stomach that can often precede vomiting.

respiratory system: A linked network of organs responsible for inhaling and distributing oxygen to the body, and exhaling waste carbon dioxide. The system of organs responsible for breathing.

surgery: A method of medical treatment that involves using tools to cut into or otherwise manipulate a patient's body.

sedative: A type of drug that causes calmness in the patient.

toxicity: The amount of harm a substance is able to cause the body.

FOR MORE INFORMATION

BOOKS

Alter, Judy. *Surgery*.
North Mankato, MN: Cherry Lake Publishing, 2013.

Burgdorf, Stephen. *Anesthetics*.
North Mankato, MN: ABDO Publishing Company, 2013.

MacDonald, Fiona. *You Wouldn't Want To Live Without Dentists!*
New York: Scholastic, 2015.

WEBSITES

www.kids.frontiersin.org/

Frontiers for Young Minds is a nonprofit scientific journal written for kids by scientists.

www.sciencekids.co.nz/

Science and technology website for kids.

Publisher's note to educators and parents: Our editors have carefully reviewed these websites to ensure that they are suitable for students. Many websites change frequently, however, and we cannot guarantee that a site's future contents will continue to meet our high standards of quality and educational value. Be advised that students should be closely supervised whenever they access the Internet.

INDEX